The Mississippi Burning Case: The History and Legacy of the Freedom Summer Murders at the Height of the Civil Rights Movement

By Charles River Editors

Portraits of the victims: James Chaney, Andrew Goodman, and Michael Schwerner

About Charles River Editors

Charles River Editors provides superior editing and original writing services across the digital publishing industry, with the expertise to create digital content for publishers across a vast range of subject matter. In addition to providing original digital content for third party publishers, we also republish civilization's greatest literary works, bringing them to new generations of readers via ebooks.

Sign up here to receive updates about free books as we publish them, and visit Our Kindle Author Page to browse today's free promotions and our most recently published Kindle titles.

Introduction

The Philadelphia Murders (June 1964)

"You see, I know what's gonna happen! I feel it deep in my heart! When they find the people who killed these guys in Neshoba County, you've got to come back to the state of Mississippi and have a jury of their cousins, their aunts and their uncles. And I know what they're going to say - not guilty."– Dave Dennis, leader of the Congress of Racial Equality (CORE)

Today every American is taught about watershed moments in the history of minorities' struggles for civil rights over the course of American history: the Civil War, *Brown v. Board of Education*, Rosa Parks' refusal to give up her seat, Dr. Martin Luther King, Jr.'s "I Have a Dream" speech, and the passage of the Civil Rights Act of 1964. Indeed, the use of the phrase "Civil Rights Movement" in America today almost invariably refers to the period of time from 1954-1964.

Even with those successes, tragedies continued to be pervasive, and one of the most notorious crimes was the murder of three civil rights workers in Philadelphia, Mississippi in June 1964. Occurring less than 2 weeks before the landmark Civil Rights Act of 1964 was passed, the young volunteers were killed because they had come south to help register blacks to vote, a right they had been unfairly denied for over half a century thanks to Jim Crow.

Fortunately, as was often the case, the shocking nature of the crimes galvanized people and helped bring about the kinds of changes the murderers sought to prevent, but despite the national outrage generated by the disappearance of the volunteers, Mississippi showed no interest in prosecuting anyone. Ultimately, the federal investigation, dubbed "Mississippi Burning," uncovered evidence of a large conspiracy that went all the way up to County Sheriff Lawrence A. Rainey, but without anyone's cooperation, the government's indictments could only bring up members of the conspiracy on minor charges. In the end, it would not be until 40 years after the murders that any of the conspirators would be tried for murder or manslaughter; that case, against 80 year old Edgar Ray Killen, also marked the first time Mississippi tried anyone for anything related to the infamous crimes.

The Mississippi Burning Case: The History and Legacy of the Notorious Murders at the Height of the Civil Rights Movement chronicles the murderous conspiracy and the aftermath. Along with pictures of important people, places, and events, you will learn about the murders like never before, in no time at all.

The Mississippi Burning Case: The History and Legacy of the Freedom Summer Murders at the Height of the Civil Rights Movement

Chapter 1: "Invaders"

"Our guess is that many of the invaders will be surprised to learn that the rank and file of Mississippi Negroes are far more intelligent than is commonly believed in areas from whence cometh these self-important missionaries for 'civil rights.' And it will probably come as a shock for them to learn that many Negroes who are registered voters didn't bother to vote in our recent elections which found a number of colored candidates seeking major offices. Quite a few of the student invaders have preconceived notions about Mississippi...hound dogs sleeping in the dust and under shade trees along Capitol Street...almost everybody illiterate, ragged, backward, living in hovels, eating sowbelly and cornpone three times daily...toting shotguns and plotting secession.... In turn, Mississippians have preconceived notions about the invading students -- smug, shrill know-it-all extroverts with a savior complex...problem brats defiant of parental restraint...sexually promiscuous, addicted to interracial love-making...brainwashed in Communist doctrines with no clear idea of Americanism...more hostile to the White South than to Red Russia.... While professing to believe in 'equality,' these self appointed reformers evidently regard themselves as mentally and morally superior to Mississippians. What the students think of us is not very important...because the invaders couldn't possibly think less of us than the majority here thinks of them and their sponsors..." - Tom Ethridge, *Jackson Clarion-Ledger*

The Civil Rights Movement was nearing its apex in the summer of 1964. A year removed from Martin Luther King's iconic "I Have a Dream" speech in the nation's capital, and coming in the wake of President Kennedy's assassination, civil rights workers were gearing up for a "Freedom Summer" that would not only seek passage of a comprehensive civil rights bill but also register minorities to vote ahead of the presidential election that fall.

In conjunction with that goal, the Student Non-Violent Coordinating Committee (SNCC) sent more than 600 young, idealistic students into one of the most segregated states in the country that summer. Sponsored by the Council of Federated Organizations (COFO), the initiative was called the Freedom Summer Project, but in hindsight, the initiative's leaders would be forced to admit that they didn't entirely know just what their efforts would entail. Bob Moses, the director of the Mississippi Summer Project, explained, "When you're not in Mississippi, it's not real. And when you're there, the rest of the world isn't real."

Moses

Conversely, for those accustomed to living and working in the Deep South, the potential for trouble was much clearer. During a speech given to those being sent south from around the country, one of the only four African American lawyers then working in Mississippi warned the volunteers, "You're going to be classified into two groups in Mississippi: n****** and n*****-lovers, and they're tougher on n***** lovers."

It also fell to Justice Department Assistant Attorney General for Civil Rights John Doar to brief the students on the situation they were walking into. He had to tell them, "There is no federal police force—the responsibility for protection is that of the local police." However, he was surprised by their reaction, recalling: "They were hostile. I hadn't thought through their likely reception to my comments. When the students started to hammer me, I thought I'd been set up a little. ...the SNCC kids were pushing hard to get the federal government into a position of protecting students."

A picture of Doar (right) escorting James Meredith to the University of Mississippi

Due to the separation of powers guaranteed in the United States Constitution, this was not possible, but at the same time, Doar assured them, "I admire what you intend to do. The real heroes in this country today are the students and particularly those students who have given their time and energy to correct the very bad and evil problems in the South with respect to the way in which American Negro citizens are treated before the law." Of course, there was no way for him to know that within a week he'd be investigating the disappearance of three of the bright eyed young people listening to him that sunny June day.

As fate would have it, this was just the beginning of surprises for the students. For many of the volunteers, the summer of 1964 would change how they looked at the country and even at the people they were trying to help. Volunteer Karin Kunstler later admitted, "Spending a summer in Mississippi taught me a lot about this country. My high school social studies teacher taught me that we all have rights. Mississippi summer taught me that we didn't all have rights. Even walking down the street in an interracial group was kind of a no-no. I remember being arrested and being asked a lot of questions. And the question that sits in my mind is the sheriff wanted me to describe the size of black men's penises. They were obsessed with sex. I don't think we were obsessed with sex. But it was a clear message that's all they thought we were doing. ... The work was frustrating. There was a very small return for the number of doors we knocked on. You could see in people's faces the struggle they were going through. Many really wanted to register but were fearful. 'I'm not going to register to vote because I work for a white family, and I think they might fire me.' Or 'I've heard that houses get burned down when people go to register to vote.' Or 'I'm worried about my kids.' We were doing something very positive but also in the backs of our minds was the negative that could befall someone we were talking to. Cause the danger was real. It was absolutely real."

Fellow organizer Julian Bond echoed those sentiments, but he acknowledged the importance of having the volunteers head to Mississippi: "When we began to go to Mississippi, the black people we met there were not interested in lunch counters. They weren't interested in sitting in the front of the bus. There were no lunch counters. There were no buses. They wanted to vote. ... The common theory about Mississippi was that you could not attack Mississippi from the inside. It had to be attacked from the outside. You had to stand away and say, 'This is an awful place and it ought to fix itself.' But Bob Moses and the Student Nonviolent Coordinating Committee said, 'That's not true. We can do it ourselves.' ... We met this cadre of older people who had been fighting. They were eager for our help and glad we were there. ... The, the genius of the Freedom Summer is that these volunteers were spread all over the state. The Freedom Summer workers are everywhere. They are in almost every little big town, almost every place where you can go, they are there. ... If you got in any kind of trouble at all, or if anybody was threatening to you, there was nobody you could go to and say 'help me.' You couldn't go to the police, you couldn't go to the sheriff, you couldn't go to the state officials. All of these people were hostile and probably the people who were threatening you, themselves. So there was nobody you could appeal to."

Perhaps the most difficult obstacles came not from outside the African American community but from inside of it. Centuries of discrimination could not be changed overnight, nor could the way minorities reacted to it. Charlie Cobb observed, "Political participation was something reserved for whites, and if blacks sought it they could get hurt in lots of different ways ranging from economic reprisals, loss of jobs, or if you had a business, restrictions are being placed on your business, or if you had a loan, your loan being called in. ... What we were trying to do was to organize these communities to take possession of their own lives. For the last hundred years the ability of black people to control their own destiny had been taken away from them. ... You're sitting on front porches, or you're walking out into a cotton field, or maybe you're at the juke joint having a beer. What we were doing was embedding ourselves in these communities. ... Immediately, what you found out you were dealing with was fear. ... We did not get a large number of people to try and register to vote, and then if within that small group of people who did try and register to vote, very few of them actually got registered to vote. They would say, 'You're right, boy. We should be registered to vote, but I ain't goin' down there to mess with 'em white people.'"

One of the most notorious things standing in the way of African Americans voting was the dreaded Literacy Test, an exam with questions so complicated that almost no one could pass it. The registrar decided which section of the Constitution each person received so that he could control the difficulty of the questions, and the final question was very subjective, leaving much of its grading in the hands of the registrar. For example, here were problems on one of the tests:

"18. WRITE AND COPY IN THE SPACE BELOW SECTION OF THE CONSTITUTION OF MISSISSIPPI [Instruction to registrar: You will designate the section of the Constitution and point out same to applicant]:

"19. WRITE IN THE SPACE BELOW A REASONABLE INTERPRETATION (THE MEANING) OF THE SECTION OF THE CONSTITUTION OF MISSISSIPPI WHICH YOU HAVE JUST COPIED:

"20. WRITE IN THE SPACE BELOW A STATEMENT SETTING FORTH YOUR UNDERSTANDING OF THE DUTIES AND OBLIGATIONS OF CITIZENSHIP UNDER A CONSTITUTIONAL FORM OF GOVERNMENT:"

Peggy Jean Connor, one of the early activists, eventually got to vote, but she described the uphill battle she faced against the test. "I just made up my mind that I was going to be a registered voter. I never wanted to be a politician. I just wanted the right to vote. … We had people who taught in colleges. We had people with the Ph.D, Master degrees and all, and they couldn't pass it. You had to be white. … Those students helped us get people registered. We registered thousands of 'em. I guess people were just fed up. People were hunting you to register to vote. You didn't have to just go to their houses. They wanted to put their name on 'em.''

Chapter 2: Assault on the Racial Barriers of Mississippi

"The president should now use the force of his office to attack the cause of the trouble in Mississippi. That trouble is the unjustified, uncalled for invasion of that sovereign state by a bunch of Northern students schooled in advance in causing trouble under the guise of bringing 'freedom' to Mississippi Negroes. An editorial in the Harvard Crimson, which was given wide circulation in Mississippi, declared that 'this summer will witness a massive, daring, probably bloody assault on the racial barriers of Mississippi.' Central to the project, the editorial said, is 'the anticipated lawlessness of Mississippi whites. The planners reason that massive non-violence will precipitate a crisis of violence which they consider a prerequisite for further progress.' The invasion of these young busybodies therefore was planned far in advance and, incredibly, has the support of the National Council of Churches. The students were schooled in invasion at Western College for Women in Oxford, Ohio. The Chicago Tribune [said] they were even taught 'how to fall if pushed off lunch counter stools and how to lock themselves into a bundle and make themselves harder to drag away.' One of the lecturers at the school was a gentleman from the Department of Justice who was booed when he told the invaders that the federal government would not promise to protect them. So there you have it. An 'invasion' planned in advance with the announced strategy of creating trouble." - *Dallas Morning News*

Most of the students who went to Mississippi that summer would return home in a few months to lives that would continue on as they mostly had, and their names would soon be forgotten, if they were ever even briefly known, by history. It turned out they were the lucky ones, because three of the volunteers would forever be remembered as martyrs to a cause they were barely old enough to fully understand.

The first of these volunteers was 24 year old Michael Schwerner, who had grown up in New York and been recruited while in college to join the Congress of Racial Equality. He had been with the organization for about six months and had already worked in Mississippi, having returned north in order to recruit and train other volunteers. Schwerner was in a hurry to return to Mississippi to look into the burning of a black church in nearby Longdale that he had previously worked with, and his widow Rita remembered, "At the end of the first week we got a call in Oxford, people at the Mt. Zion Church had been beaten up badly and the church was burned. My husband Mickey and James Chaney decided that they needed to go right away to see how people were and to provide whatever support they could. Andy Goodman was going to be one of the volunteers working in Meridian out of the Meridian office so they decided that all three of them would go. We were in the dorm room that we had been assigned, and Mickey kissed me goodbye and said, 'I'll see you at the end of the week,' and left. And they drove down in the blue station wagon."

Schwerner

Rita

James Chaney was a 21 year old who had been assigned to Schwerner as his aide. Unlike most of the others, Chaney was from the South and had volunteered for the Summer Project to try to improve the lives of his friends, family, and others he hoped to someday meet.

Chaney

Andrew Goodman, only 20 years old, had been recruited by Schwerner from the Upper West Side of Manhattan. When he told his mother that he was going to Mississippi, he insisted it was "because it is the most important thing going on in the country."

Goodman

The three young men left Ohio early on Sunday morning, June 20, ahead of the main group, and they started driving south. Young and energetic, they drove straight through to Meridian, where Goodman dashed off a quick letter to his parents: "Dear Mom and Dad, I have arrived safely in Meridian, Mississippi. This is a wonderful town and the weather is fine. I wish you were here. The people in this city are wonderful and our reception was very good. All my love, Andy."

In Meridian, the three got some sleep and breakfast before heading out for Longdale and the burned remains of the church Schwerner wanted to see, but they would never make it. Dave Dennis, one of the organizers that summer, recalled the feeling of dread that engulfed him when he heard the three were missing: "It was close around six or seven o'clock, around six or seven o'clock in the evening, and a call came in from the Meridian people. They had not heard from Mickey and James Chaney. I just knew that something had to be wrong."

At first, no one mentioned their concerns to Rita, hoping that it would turn out that the workers had just had car trouble or some other delay, but as the hours continued to pass, she had to be told. She immediately thought the worst: "It was early Monday morning around one or two in the morning when someone came to the dorm room that I was using, and woke me to say that the men had not returned, and that was how I first heard of it. I urged people to contact their families and have their families contact their congressional people, to indicate that we believe there certainly was a possibility -- given the fact that so many hours had gone by and that they couldn't be located -- that they might've been killed."

John Doar also got a call in the wee hours of Monday morning; Mary King was calling from the office of the Student Nonviolent Coordinating Committee in Atlanta to tell him that on this, the first day of the Summer Project, there was already trouble. "I was at home when I got the call from someone in Mississippi, telling me about the situation and I reported it immediately to the Federal Bureau of Investigation. And Bob Owen was in Mississippi and we, I got a hold of him and had him go right up there to Nishoba County. I can't remember when we recognized that, but I guess when the car was found, and burned at the edge of Nishoba County, it was fairly clear that the kids had been killed."

The burned station wagon

An aerial photo showing the location of the abandoned station wagon near the Bogue Chitto River

At that time, Doar's hands were still tied, so he suggested to King that she call the Mississippi Highway Safety Patrol. In the meantime, he also called the FBI to let the agency know what he feared had happened.

On Tuesday, June 22, newspapers first began to run stories about the disappearance of the three volunteers, portraying the situation as part of the larger dangers the students in the movement were facing. One *Associated Press* story told readers, "COFO said today three of its workers failed to return to Meridian from a trip to Philadelphia, Miss., where they had gone to investigate an alleged bombing. A spokesman said the absence of the bi-racial group had been reported to local authorities in the central Mississippi towns and also the FBI. Reported missing were Mickey Schwerner, New York: Andy Goodman, Queens, New. York: and James Chancy, Meridian, a Negro. The COFO spokesman said the three left Meridian 'sometime Sunday' and were expected back in that city about 4 p.m. He said they had intended to go to Philadelphia, about 35 miles away, to investigate the bombing reported by a church near Philadelphia last week. Police in Meridian and Philadelphia would not comment on the COFO report, including whether they had received a missing persons report."

The word of the trio's disappearance had quickly spread back to Ohio, where the orientation was still going on. Gwendolyn Zoharah Simmons, one of the volunteers there that day, remembered, "Everybody was to come into the auditorium for this session. They had this extremely solemn look on their faces, and then they told us that three workers who had been at the orientation and had left early, they had disappeared. ... Learning that three of our members, two of whom were white, had disappeared really blew away all my ideas that possibly we would have protection from the fact that the majority of the summer volunteers were white. I knew now that that was not the case: that everybody was in grave danger, and that these Mississippians would kill all of us, white and black."

The people working on the project also had to grapple with what to do next. Should the project be called off and no more students sent out until the men were found, or should those involved carry on as planned? Linda Wetmore Halpern admitted there was no easy answer: "Bob said that, 'There is no guarantee that you will get out of this summer alive, so just know that. It's up to you if you want to continue on.' So he left us all to the phones, and we all went. We were told to call home. ... My mother and father did not ask me to come home. They asked me to do what I thought was right. So I boarded the buses."

More details were gleaned locally in Mississippi, though not surprisingly, the whole picture was not revealed. Just before 7:00 a.m. on Monday morning, June 22, Minnie Herring, an employee with the Neshoba County Jail, told someone calling from the Program's office in Jackson, Mississippi that Schwerner and the others had been arrested the previous afternoon for speeding. She said they had spent a few hours at the jail, where they had eaten supper and paid a fine of $25 before being released. When questioned, Sheriff Lawrence Rainey confirmed this.

Sheriff Rainey

By this time, Doar had decided to involve the FBI, and Special Agent John Proctor, assigned to Meridian, began investigating the volunteers' disappearance. He began by interviewing a number of African Americans who lived near the Mount Zion church, but they were reluctant to help for fear of their own safety. Proctor also spoke with Rainey and Deputy Cecil Price, with the latter telling him that after he arrested the three, he heard "they had spent the day in the neighborhood of that burned-out n***** church. I figured they might have had something to do with the church-burning." When they finished talking, Price cheerfully took a bottle of confiscated liquor out of the trunk of his patrol car and said, "Hell, John, let's have a drink."

Rainey (foreground) and Price

As the mystery deepened, the press descended on the small town of Philadelphia, with one reporter doing a rather disturbing "person on the street" interview:

> "Reporter: Late this afternoon the search for Chaney, Goodman, and Schwerner shifted to the Pearl River near Philadelphia, Mississippi. Boats carrying Game Wardens and FBI Agents are now dragging the river. … What do you think of this?
>
> Mississippi man: I believe them jokers planned it and they're sittin' there in New York, laughing at us Mississippians.

Reporter: Can you tell me what you think of this whole thing?

Mississippi woman: Well I think it's a big publicity hoax, but if they're dead I feel like they asked for it."

Of course, there were family members back home for whom the investigation was the only thing that mattered. Organizer Julian Bond explained, "Rita Schwerner plays an important role here. This is her husband after all who is the leader of the three missing men, and she puts a face on them, and she plays an enormous role in making this seem like these are real people and we need to pay attention to these real people who something terrible has happened to. … There's this great pressure within the movement, people saying, 'Well, we did our best. We did the right thing and it didn't work out. You know, when we were organizers, that was okay, but when we tried to have power, the power rose up and, and knocked us down.'"

Dorothy Zellner described Rita's interactions with the media: "The press swarmed all over her, and I think they wanted her to cry, and they wanted her to be a new widow, that they would catch her at the moment of her widow-hood, and she wouldn't play."

Instead, Rita insisted that her husband was still alive and she would find him: "They're being held somewhere, or something happened, and I am going to find the answer. If this means driving every back road, every dirt road, every alley in the county of Neshoba, I will do it. I personally suspect that if Mr. Chaney who is a native Mississippian negro had been alone at the time of the disappearance, that this case, like so many others who have come before, would have gone completely unnoticed."

True to form, Rita was just as vocal even when she was introduced to President Johnson, telling him directly, "Mr. President, this is not a social call. I've come to find out where my husband is." Johnson later complained to FBI Director J. Edgar Hoover that Rita "was awfully mean, and very ugly. She came in this afternoon and she wants thousands of extra people put down there and said I'm the only one that has the authority to do it. I told her I'd put all that we could efficiently handle and I was going to let you determine how many we could efficiently handle."

Johnson

Hoover

Chapter 3: They Wouldn't Care to Cooperate

"A week ago there was some talk around the courthouse about three so-called civil rights workers being arrested for speeding. After they had posted bail, a deputy sheriff had followed them part of the way back to Meridian. The old men, long experts of the courthouse talk, first heard from local officials of the three having disappeared. ... The trio (were) unknown locally, and who know which way they might have gone when they left Philadelphia. Then Monday a burned station wagon, used by the three, was found about 12 miles northeast of town. Since that time Philadelphia has led most news stories all over the world. During the past seven days, Neshoba Countians have seen hundreds of federal agents, highway patrol personnel, and even members of the U.S. Navy trampling over the countryside. They have heard the President of the United States talk about their town. They have read about a visit by Allen Dulles to Mississippi to discuss their town. They have seen one of the largest groups of news media personnel ever to gather in Mississippi. They have seen their town Philadelphia, through the eyes of national television; they have heard about their town on radio; they have seen their town through the 'eyes' of newsprint and pictures. ... An inquirer gets the feeling that these Mississippians don't know what happened to the three. And after the treatment they have received from national news media, they wouldn't care to cooperate with visiting television folk." - *Jackson Clarion-Ledger*, June 30, 1964

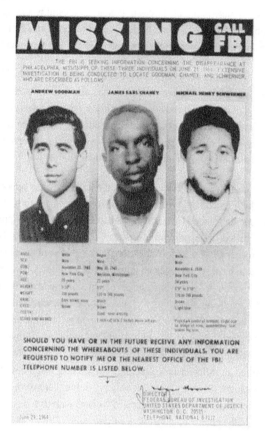

As people across the country speculated, some progress was being made gradually and grudgingly. One of the things that Proctor learned during his preliminary investigation was that the missing men had not been released at 6:00 p.m. that night but closer to 10:00 p.m., and they had last been seen driving south out of Philadelphia on Highway 19. Doar also learned that the State Patrol had issued an all-points bulletin on them.

Even with this information, the question remained as to whether or not the FBI could justify stepping in, and Doar finally won this point when the Justice Department announced that it would be treating the case as a kidnapping, allowing them to step in under the "Lindbergh Law."

On Tuesday, June 23, President Lyndon Johnson was asked about the disappearance during a press conference, and he told the public, "The FBI has a substantial number of men who are closely studying and investigating the entire situation. We have asked them to spare no effort to secure all of the information possible, and report to us as soon as possible. We believe that they are making every effort to locate them. I have had no reports since breakfast, but at that time I understood that they had increased their forces in that area. Several weeks ago I had asked them to anticipate the problems that would come from this, and to send extra FBI personnel into the area. They have substantially augmented their personnel in the last few hours."

In fact, by that time, Johnson had been informed that the workers' car had been found in a swamp northeast of Philadelphia. Moreover, Hoover had also told the president that the car had been so badly burned that it was still too hot to examine. Even as he was given this information, the legendary FBI Director remained a thorn in the president's side, as he confided to Attorney General Bobby Kennedy and others: "There are three sovereignties involved. There's the United States, there's the State of Mississippi, and there's J. Edgar Hoover."

The good news was that Hoover had long been on the lookout for an opportunity to investigate the Ku Klux Klan, which federal authorities believed was almost certainly involved in the case, and eventually, Johnson dispatched CIA Director Allen Dulles to Mississippi to head up the investigation. Doar recalled, "[Department of Justice Civil Rights Division Director] Burke Marshall came into my office, at 6, or 7 o'clock, or 10 o'clock one night and said that the President had decided to have Alan Dulles go down, the head of the CIA to make an investigation of the situation in Mississippi and give his recommendations. And Mr. Dulles came to the Justice Department the next morning and, the Attorney General had me come up and talk to him because I was more familiar with Mississippi than most anyone, probably anybody else in the department. And I went to Mississippi with Alan Dulles and out of that trip, the Justice Department made a recommendation that the FBI increase its force in Mississippi substantially. And Mr. Hoover opened an office in Jackson and put some very excellent FBI investigators in charge of that investigation. And they were not only good, but there were a lot of them and they worked all that summer and solved that murder and worked with us to present to a grand jury and to a regular jury trial of the people responsible for those deaths."

Dulles

Upon arriving in Mississippi, Dulles and Doar met first with Governor Paul Johnson, who somehow told them with a straight face that "there is complete tranquility between the races" in Mississippi. The governor had already gone on record as speculating that the missing men were likely hiding out, perhaps in Cuba, in order to get publicity. Needless to say, he was not particularly helpful, especially after the Bureau landed an army of investigators in the Mississippi town and its environs.

Johnson

Likewise, most of those in the dominant white community did not welcome federal investigators into their state. On July 2, *Birmingham News* reported, "Four hundred sailors, scores of FBI agents -- employees of Uncle Sam -- push through dust, weeds, branches, mud and water not far from this national dateline. Eleven hours a day they hunt for clues of three missing men. Few Mississippians, officials or otherwise, seem to be doing very much active searching. A Mississippi highway patrolman accompanies each squad of sailors. Their mission, said Gov. Paul Johnson, is to 'be certain that the people's houses and property of this area are protected at all times.' Some state investigators, including some brass, spend a good portion of every day under a giant pecan tree behind the small Philadelphia City Hall. One top investigator, pistol on, lies stretched out in an aluminum, web lounge chair, arms up behind his head. Four or five other chairs under the sheltering tree are for other state men who come and go…. State people for the most part seem to be standing by. Federal agents carry the burden of effort to find the missing men. … Last Tuesday morning several highway patrol cars stood parked near a church to the west. Maybe more such are present than are needed. These officers only stood around talking to each other. 'We were just told to park here,' said one. The Philadelphia police chief and his assistants haven't been evident much in the searching either. Most of the time they seem busy about their duties in town…. The police chief and Philadelphia's mayor provided a small courtroom for state and federal officers, for private phone calls and conferences. Meetings between federal and state men have been increasingly few recently."

Chapter 4: Information is Close-Guarded

"The FBI, quite obviously, is keeping almost strictly to itself. Its information is close-guarded. State men give no evidence that federal agents tell them much when they do sit down together. There is a careful courtesy between local and state officers and federal investigators. But there is an obvious distance between them too. State people appear to feel that the FBI ought to be confiding more in them. Equally apparent, the FBI -- which usually says as little as possible -- seems to feel its facts are best kept to itself. 'Cooperation' in Neshoba County is more ritual than reality. Gov. Johnson of Mississippi has said, 'this [search] is a joint effort. This is a cooperative effort between local, state and federal agents. . . .' The federal agents do not mix. They attend to their business and mind their tongues. They are quartered in a small motel due west of Philadelphia. They do not tarry long at City Hall when they must visit it. Monday a federal agent pulled his car up to park near City Hall. His vehicle blocked a woman clerk's car as she worked inside. A state man suggested someone ought to tell the agent, so he could move his car. 'Wait until he's walked up here,' said another state officer under the pecan tree. 'This is a cooperative effort,' the governor had said." - *Birmingham News*, July 2, 1964

Lyndon Johnson signing the Civil Rights Act on July 2, 1964

By the beginning of July, the FBI agents were sure they were looking for bodies, not men, and Bob Moses had broken the news to the other volunteers that the three were in all likelihood deceased. However, no bodies were found near the burned car, and the search for the workers, or at least their remains, continued on in the heat of the Mississippi summer, causing more than one agent to wonder how he had ended up in such a hostile, unpleasant environment where the mosquitoes were friendlier than the citizens.

Things got even more interesting when Hoover himself showed up. On July 10, President Johnson told reporters, "The information I have on Mr. Hoover's visit is that he has recently added additional FBI personnel to his force in Mississippi, some additional 50 agents. After a survey of the situation he has decided that he should establish a headquarters office in that State, that he is transferring a director from out of State, an assistant director to take charge of that office, that they have made arrangements for the new office to be opened, and that he will officially open it sometime today. Of course, I am told that while he is there he will confer with the responsible people from his service who have been stationed there for some time, and get a complete report and give any instructions that he may think are indicated to the people under his jurisdiction."

Tragically, the FBI's search turned up a number of bodies of missing civil rights workers that summer - those that had lain for months in swamps or shallow, unmarked graves - but they still did not find Schwerner, Goodman, or Chaney. Thus, after more than a month of searching, Doar decided to change his tactics and focus more on investigating the men's last hours, working under the assumption that they had been killed by people who knew the area and could make sure their bodies were never found. So, he reasoned, he would just have to get enough evidence together on someone to force him to confess. To that end, he began to send agents out to interview anyone and everyone that might know something about the case, eventually logging in interviews with more than 1,000 people, half of whom were somehow connected with the Klan.

Finally, the FBI hit pay dirt, figuratively and literally, when an anonymous citizen responded to the $30,000 reward by telling them where they would find the bodies. On August 4, the FBI ordered a bulldozer to begin tearing down an earthen dam on Old Jolly Farm, and by the end of the day, they had the three bodies they were looking for. Mississippi resident Roscoe Jones remembered, "On August 4th, 1964 at the Mt. Olive Missionary Baptist Church in Meridian, Mississippi Pete Seeger gave a concert. You know, we were all into James Brown and all that, and here, you know, we got a guy who's a folk legend that comes to Meridian, and we were told that he's gonna do this concert. ... And, all of a sudden in the middle of a song that he was singing someone came over and whispered into his ear. He stopped, and he got up and made an announcement. ... He asked us to join hands and sing, 'We shall overcome, my Lord. We shall overcome someday. We shall overcome someday...'"

For his part, Seeger recalled, "It was a small church but everybody was standing so there were about 200 people there, and I had been singing to them I guess on a slight raised platform probably near the pulpit, and I had gotten them singing with me. ... [Then I announced] 'The bodies of Schwerner, Goodman and Chaney have just been discovered. They were buried deep in the earth.' There wasn't any shouting. There's just silence. I saw people's lips moving as though they were in prayer."

Rita described her feelings when she got the news: "I got a call late in the evening. At least this nightmare of unknowing, or at least not officially knowing, was over." As few days later, Johnson assured Americans, "I have just talked to Mr. J. Edgar Hoover, head of the Federal Bureau of Investigation. He assures me that the investigation in Mississippi is going exceedingly well; that substantive results can be expected in a very short period of time. Murder in any State, whether Mississippi or Georgia or New York, and civil disorder in any region - North or South,

East or West - cannot and will not be condoned in this country. Perpetrators of these crimes and these law violators are being apprehended and will be brought to justice. We must not allow violence and lawlessness to go unpunished. No person can be allowed to attack the right of every American to be secure in this land. Under our system of government, local authorities have the basic responsibilities for civil peace. We look to the Governors and local officials to keep the peace and to protect the citizens. It is essential to our Federal system that they keep that responsibility. I am in constant communication with Governors where these problems appear. A Federal police force is inconsistent with the tradition of this country, and I do not believe we must create such a force to keep the peace and enforce the laws. But inaction on the part of the Government when Federal laws are violated and assistance is needed is equally repugnant to our traditions. We intend to do our part when it is necessary and right to do so."

Once the bodies were found, it was time to plan a proper funeral. Goodman and Schwerner were flown back to be buried in their home state, while Chaney's body remained in his native Mississippi. Dave Dennis later said, "The decision had been made by family members and local leaders and others that they wanted to keep this very quiet and then low key, rather. I did the eulogy."

And what a eulogy it was. Stirring with rage at the ongoing injustices inflicted on minorities like Chaney and the refusal by others to do enough, Dennis told those assembled, "I'm not here to do the traditional thing most of us do at such a gathering. And that is to tell of what a great person the individual was and some of the great works the person was involved in and et cetera. I think we all know because he walked these dusty streets of Meridian and around here before I came here. With you and around you. Played with your kids and he talked to all of them. And what I want to talk about is really what I really grieve about. I don't grieve for Chaney because the fact is I feel he lived a fuller life than many of us will ever live. I feel that he's got his freedom and we are still fighting for it. Well I'm getting sick and tired! I'm sick and tired of going to memorials! I'm sick and tired of going to funerals! I've got a bitter vengeance in my heart tonight! And I'm sick and tired and can't help but feel bitter, you see, deep down inside and I'm not going to stand here and ask anybody not to be angry tonight. ... You see, I know what's gonna happen! I feel it deep in my heart! When they find the people who killed these guys in Neshoba County, you've got to come back to the state of Mississippi and have a jury of their cousins, their aunts and their uncles. And I know what they're going to say - not guilty...'And one thing that I'm worried about is just exactly what are we going to do as people as a result of what happened, for what this guy died for and the other people died for. We're going to come to this memorial here, say, 'Oh, what a shame,' go back home and pray to the Lord as we've done for years. We go back to work in some white folks' kitchen tomorrow and forget the about the whole God-blasted thing, you see. [Audience starts clapping] Don't applaud! Don't applaud! Don't get your frustration out by clapping your hands. Each and every one of us as individuals is going to have to take it upon ourself to become leaders in our community. Block by block, house by house, city by city, state by state throughout this entire country. ... For the whites in the community and those same ones you cook for, wash and iron for, who come right out and say, 'I can't sit down and eat beside a n*****,' or anything like that. I'm tired of that, you see. I'm tired of him talking about how much he hates me and he can't stand for me to go to school with his children and all of that. But yet, when he wants someone to baby-sit for him, he gets my black mammy to hold that baby! And as long as he can do that, he can sit down beside me, he can watch me go up there and register to vote, he can watch me take some type of public office in this state, and he can sit down as I rule over him just as he's ruled over me for years, you see."

By this time, the church was reeling, but Dennis aimed to stiffen everyone's resolve at the finish: "I blame the people in Washington DC and on down in the state of Mississippi just as much as I blame those who pulled the trigger. ... I'm tired of that! Another thing that makes me even tireder though, that is the fact that we as people here in the state and the country are allowing it to continue to happen. ... Don't just look at me and the people here and go back and say that you've been to a nice service, a lot of people came, there were a lot of hot-blasted newsmen around, anything like that. But your work is just beginning. I'm going to tell you deep down in my heart what I feel right now. If you do go back home and sit down and take it, God damn your souls!"

Looking back, Dennis said of his eulogy, "All the different emotions and things that had been going through, leading up to this particular moment. Began to come out, boil up in me, I call this. And then looking out and then looking up and seeing Ben Chaney. James Chaney's little brother. I lost it. I totally just lost it."

Chapter 5: A Big Circus

"Maybe the best course for everybody is just to let the bodies lie and let the excitement gradually die down. Once the bodies are found, then there is a great hue and cry to convict somebody . . . to put somebody in jail. And that's a power I don't have. That power doesn't exist in Mississippi. Not even Paul Johnson has any such power. There is no way in the world, in open court, where a twelve-man jury verdict must be unanimous, and where every juror can be polled in open court and made to say how he voted--there's no possible way to ever put anybody in jail. Instead of reducing hate, all a trial can do is spread it. So why should we have all that hue and cry, and a big circus trial, with everybody goddamming Mississippi? What's the use of it? Since a murder like this was expected, why don't we all just admit that we got what we expected and devote ourselves to trying to prevent another one?" - An unnamed Philadelphia businessman

Portraits of some of the alleged conspirators. Top Row: Lawrence A. Rainey, Bernard L. Akin, Other "Otha" N. Burkes, Olen L. Burrage, Edgar Ray Killen. Bottom Row: Frank J. Herndon, James T. Harris, Oliver R. Warner, Herman Tucker , and Samuel H. Bowers.

Now certain that the men they were looking for were indeed dead, the FBI was able to turn their attention fully to finding out who murdered them. Over the next few months they combed the highways and bi-ways of Mississippi, talking to people and going over what little bit of physical evidence they had with a fine-tooth comb. Still, it remained difficult to determine exactly what happened to the three while they were jailed, and some uncertainty persists 50 years later.

Based on what authorities believe, not long after they were booked, Deputy Cecil Price met with Edgar Ray Killen to hatch a plan to harm the men. When Schwerner asked to make a phone call, his request was refused, and it was also determined that Price followed them after he released them. Minnie Herring later testified, "Well, Price came into the jail and up in the hall to our quarters at 10:30 and said, 'Mr. Herring, Chaney wants to pay off, and he said, we'll let him pay off and we'll release them all.' Well, my husband opened the door and he walked around the white boys were in the front cell and the colored boy was on the back, so he walked around the bars and asked the colored boy if he wanted to pay off, and Chaney asked him how much was it and he told him it would be twenty dollars. Well, he didn't have the $20.00 on him so he borrowed it from Schwerner and paid the fine, and so my husband wrote the receipt and Cecil went back and unlocked the combination and let them out and walked on out in the little hall. He had their belongings in a little box, and I had their driver's license, so each one of them reached in and got their billfolds, and put their driver's license in their billfolds, and my husband gave them the receipt and Price told them, 'see how quick you all can get out of Neshoba County,' and they thanked him and went on out."

Killen

By this time, Killen had contacted a number of other people, including Horace Doyle Barnette, who, after extensive questioning during the latter days of November, finally confessed to the FBI that he was one of the men involved in the murder. "On June 21, 1964 about 8:00 P.M., I was having supper at Jimmy Arledge's house, Meridian, Mississippi. Travis Barnette called Arledge on the telephone and told Arledge that the Klan had a job and wanted to know if Arledge and I could go. Arledge asked me if I could go and we went to Akins trailer park on Highway 80 in Meridian, Miss. We did not know what the job was. Upon arriving at Akins trailer park we were met by Preacher Killen, Mr. Akins, Jim Jordan and Wayne [Roberts]. ... Killen told us that three civil rights workers were in jail in Philadelphia, Miss., and that these three civil rights workers were going to be released from jail and that we were going to catch them and give them a whipping."

Barnette (middle)

Barnette soon learned that the men he was with that night had much worse things than whipping on their minds: "When we arrived in Philadelphia, about 9:30 P.M., we met Killen and he got into my car...While we were talking, Killen stated that 'we have a place to bury them, and a man to run the dozer to cover them up.' This was the first time I realized that the three civil rights workers were to be killed."

As those men headed for the three volunteers, Price returned to Philadelphia and dropped off another officer. He then made his way quickly back to Highway 19 to pursue the station wagon. From there, Barnette and the others caught up with him, and according to Barnette, this was all part of the plan. "About 5 or 10 minutes after we parked, a patrolman from Philadelphia came to the car and said that 'they are going toward Meridian on Highway 19.' We proceeded out Highway 19 and caught up to a Mississippi State Patrol Car, who pulled into a store on the left hand side of the road. We pulled alongside of the patrol car and then another car from Philadelphia pulled in between us. ... No one got out of the cars, but the driver of the Philadelphia car, who I later learned was named Posey, talked to the patrolmen. Posey then drove away and we followed. About 2 or 3 miles down the Highway Posey's car stopped and pulled off on the right hand side of the road. Posey motioned for me to go ahead. I then drove fast and caught up to the car that the three civil rights workers were in, pulled over to the side of the road and stopped. About a minute or 2 later, Deputy Sheriff Price came along and stopped on the pavement beside my car. Jordan asked him who was going to stop them and Price said that he would and took after them and we followed. The Civil Rights workers turned off Highway 19 on to a side road and drove about a couple of miles before Price stopped them. Price stopped his car behind the 1963 Ford Fairlane Station Wagon driven by the Civil Rights Workers and we stopped behind Price's car."

Though Barnette did not mention it, later testimony indicated that at some point, Chaney, who was driving, decided to try to outrun the police cruiser. However, the station wagon never stood a chance in such a race, and after trying to lose his pursuers by turning onto Highway 492, he gave up.

From this moment on, the trio's fate was sealed. According to Barnette, "Price stated 'I thought you were going back to Meridian if we let you out of jail.' The Civil Rights Workers stated that they were and Price asked them why they were taking the long way around. Price told them to get out and get into his car. They got out of their car and proceed to get into Price's car and then Price took his blackjack and struck Chaney on the back of the head."

The men pulled off again, this time with one of them driving the victims' station wagon while they were stuck in Price's vehicle. They pulled down a lonely gravel road, where the actual murders took place. Barnette described what happened next: "Before I could get out of the car Wayne ran past my car to Price's car, opened the left rear door, pulled Schwerner out of the car, spun him around so that Schwerner was standing on the left side of the road, with his back to the ditch and said 'Are you that n***** lover' and Schwerner said 'Sir, I know just how you feel.' Wayne had a pistol in his right hand, then shot Schwerner. Wayne then went back to Price's car and got Goodman, took him to the left side of the road with Goodman facing the road, and shot Goodman. … Schwerner fell to the left so that he was laying alongside the road. Goodman spun around and fell back toward the bank in back. At this time Jim Jordan said 'save one for me.' He then got out of Price's car and got Chaney out. I remember Chaney backing up, facing the road, and standing on the bank on the other side of the ditch and Jordan stood in the middle of the road and shot him. … Jordan then said. 'You didn't leave me anything but a n*****, but at least I killed me a n*****.'"

Other testimony would later contradict Barnette on the issue of who shot who. James Jordan claimed that Roberts shot all three men and that Barnette also shot Chaney twice.

Regardless of who shot which victim, the posse began to work on disposing the bodies and the car. Barnette asserted, "The three civil rights workers were then put into the back of their 1963 Ford wagon. …Price then got into his car and drove back toward Highway 19. Wayne, Posey and Jordan then got into the 1963 Ford and started up the road. Snowden, Arledge and another person who I do not know the name of got into my car and we followed…went through the outskirts of Philadelphia and to the Dam site on Burrage's property…When we arrived at the Dam site someone said that the bulldozer operator was not there and Wayne, Arledge and I went in my car to find him. We drove out to a paved road and about a mile down the road. … Wayne told me to stop and we backed up to this car. Burrage and 2 other men were in the car. Wayne said that they were already down there and Burrage said to follow them. ... Burrage said 'it is just a little ways over there,' and Wayne and the bulldozer operator walked the rest of the way. ... Arledge and I then followed Burrage and the other man back to Burrage's garage. ...Burrage got a glass gallon jug and filled it with gasoline to be used to burn the 1963 Ford car owned by the three civil rights workers. ... It was then about 1:00 to 1:30 in the morning. Snowden, Arledge, Jordan, Wayne and I then got into my car and we drove back toward Philadelphia. When we got to Philadelphia a city patrol car stopped us and we got out. Sheriff Rainey, Deputy Sheriff Price and the City Patrolman, who told us which way the civil rights workers were leaving town, got out of the patrol car. ... We talked for 2 or 3 minutes and then someone said that we better not talk about this and Sheriff Rainey said 'I'll kill anyone who talks, even if it was my own brother.' We then got back into my car and drove back to Meridian..."

Portraits of the alleged lynch mob. Top Row, L-R: Cecil R. Price, Travis M. Barnette, Alton W. Roberts, Jimmy K. Arledge, Jimmy Snowden. Bottom Row, L-R: Jerry M. Sharpe, Billy W. Posey, Jimmy L. Townsend, Horace D. Barnette, James Jordan.

Chapter 6: So Many Theories

"Now, what's the theory of the Government's case? Actually isn't it a theory of this case that here in Mississippi, that there is so much hate and prejudice in Mississippi that we hate all outsiders, and that there is a group of people here in Mississippi so filled with that hate that they conspire together and meet together [and] organize organizations to do away and murder outsiders that come into this State. ...all the times I've been engaged in the practice of law I never knew a State of a Government in the presentation of their case to try to blow hot and cold in the same breath. They got in here and they put Jim Jordan on the stand and he sat up there with his eyes all bugged out and he just rattles it off like that, just exactly what happened, he said. Then, the government, just a little bit later, brings statement and say you ought to convict somebody on which impeaches almost everything he said. I just don't see how the government can have so many theories of these cases and then represent to you there's no reasonable doubts, there's no mistake." - H. C. Wilkins

Less than two weeks after Barnette confessed, FBI agents served warrants on 19 men accused of collaborating in the murders of the young civil rights workers. All of them were Klan members, and several of them were law enforcement officers. Barnette, who by this time had recanted his confession, was also arrested.

However, since murder was a state crime, and thus something over which the FBI had no jurisdiction, the men were charged with the federal crime of "conspiring to violate the civil rights…under color of state law." Actual murder charges could only come from Mississippi, and not surprisingly, those were not forthcoming anytime soon.

Furthermore, the federal government's charges failed to hold up for even a week. Just six days later, Commissioner Esther Carter of the United States Commissioner for the Southern District of Mississippi dismissed the charges, ruling that Barnette's confession constituted only hearsay evidence and therefore was not admissible.

After that setback, Doar and the others took the case to a federal grand jury in Jackson, and this time, in February 1965, Judge William Harold Cox dismissed all the indictments except those against Price and Rainey, determining that none of the other men had acted "under color of state law." The prosecution appealed, and a year later, in March 1966, the United States Supreme Court ruled, "The present application of the statutes at issue does not raise fundamental questions of federal-state relationships. We are here concerned with allegations which squarely and indisputably involve state action in direct violation of the mandate of the Fourteenth Amendment -- that no State shall deprive any person of life or liberty without due process of law. This is a direct, traditional concern of the Federal Government. It is an area in which the federal interest has existed for at least a century, and in which federal participation has intensified as part of a renewed emphasis upon civil rights. Even as recently as 1951, when Williams I was decided, the federal role in the establishment and vindication of fundamental rights -- such as the freedom to travel, nondiscriminatory access to public areas and nondiscriminatory educational facilities -- was neither as pervasive nor as intense as it is today. Today, a decision interpreting a federal law in accordance with its historical design, to punish denials by state action of constitutional rights of the person can hardly be regarded as adversely affecting 'the wise adjustment between State responsibility and national control . . . .' In any event, the problem, being statutory and not constitutional, is ultimately, as it was in the beginning, susceptible of congressional disposition."

Cox

Following this decision, the defense tried to allege, in what can only be one of the most egregious uses of irony in American history, that the first indictments were suspect because the grand jury issuing them did not have enough minorities. Instead of being sucked into arguing this point, the government seated a new grand jury and, on the last day of February 1967, won new indictments. This time, there were 18 Klansmen accused.

When the trial finally began on Monday, October 9, 1967, 350 men and women gathered together to see if they would be chosen to as part of the jury. At Doar's request, they came from the entire Southern Mississippi District, not just the six counties around Neshoba. Judge Cox, who had previously had his decision on the indictments overturned, was determined to have order and made sure that no cameras made it into his courtroom. In front of the judge sat a total of 15 lawyers - Doar and two others on the prosecution's side, and every member of the Neshoba County Bar Association on the other.

The jury was seated with surprising speed, as Doar explained, "We were looking for signs of intelligence. I had my guys look at everybody's homes—we were looking for homes that were well kept up." There were seven women and five men, all of them white; the 17 African Americans who had been called were all struck by the defense.

The trial began in earnest on Tuesday, when Doar stood to make his opening statements. He told the jurors, "I hope very much that you will understand the reason I have come here. It's not because of any skilled experience that I am here, but only because I hold the office as head of the division with the Department of Justice, and it is my responsibility to try and enforce the law in which these defendants have been charged. The United States Government felt it was essential that one of its Washington officials be here to speak directly and frankly to you about the reason for the extraordinary effort the Federal Government undertook to solve this crime, and to state to you twelve Jurors why the Federal Government has assumed the role of prosecutor of this conspiracy involving murder. ... When local law enforcement officials become involved as participants in violent crime and use their position, power and authority to accomplish this, there is very little to be hoped for, except with assistance from the Federal Government. But members of the jury, exactly what does that mean? It means that the Federal Government is not invading Philadelphia or Neshoba County, Mississippi. It means only that these defendants are tried for a crime under Federal law in a Mississippi city, before a Mississippi federal judge, in a Mississippi courtroom before twelve men and women from the State of Mississippi. The sole responsibility of the determination of guilt or innocence of these men remain in the hands where it should remain, the hands of twelve citizens from the State of Mississippi."

Doar's first witness was the Reverend Charles Johnson, who spoke of Mickey Schwerner's work in the area. His should have been a pretty simple testimony since it had nothing to do with the actual case, but defense attorney Laurel Weir turned it into a bombshell when he asked the witness, "Now, let me ask you if you and Mr. Schwerner didn't advocate and try to get young male negroes to sign statements agreeing to rape a white woman once a week during the hot summer of 1964?" The prosecution objected and Judge Cox took great offense at the question, leading to the following damaging exchange:

"COX: Who wrote the question? Whose question is it?

"ALFORD: Brother Killen wrote the question, one of the defendants.

"COX: One of the defendants wrote the question? All right, I'm going to expect some basis for that question since Counsel has adopted one of the defendant's questions and if there's no basis for it, when I get through I'm going to say something about that. ... I'm not going to allow a farce to be made of this trial and everybody might as well get that through their heads including everyone of these defendants right now.

"WEIR: Your Honor please, I will be more careful from now on about the questions I ask and I do beg the Court to understand that on this particular occasion I was trying to be diligent in obeying the Court's orders you know.

"COX: I don't understand such a question as that, and I don't appreciate it, and I'm going to say so before I get through with the trial of this case. So you can govern yourselves accordingly and you can act just as reckless as you want to in asking questions like that. Go along. ... I'm surprised at a question like that coming from a preacher too, I'm talking about Killen, or whatever his name is..."

Doar recalled the effect the question had: "The rape question was a tremendous blunder. It was the second big turning point. If there had been any feeling in the courtroom that the defendants were invulnerable to conviction in Mississippi, the incident dispelled it completely. Cox made it clear he was taking the trial seriously. That made the jurors stop and think: 'If Judge Cox is taking this stand, we'd better meet our responsibility as well.'"

Over the coming days, Doar and the others built their case slowly, piece by piece. Ernest Kirkland testified that he had met with the men on the day they were killed concerning the recent church fire. State Patrolman E. R. Poe admitted he had heard Price cry out gleefully, "I've got a good one!" about 15 minutes before seeing Price with the men on the side of the road as they changed a tire on the station wagon. Dr. William Featherstone testified that the men had been shot, the white men through their hearts and Chaney in the head.

The most damning witnesses were three Klan members who testified about the extensive plans that had been made in the days leading up to the murders to at least do something to harm the arriving activists. Doar later told the jury, "To understand this case, you must understand the White Knights of the Ku Klux Klan. In seeking members, the White Knights are reported to be a political organization, a non-violent, peaceful group, but once the members were inducted, once the oath was administered, the members soon learned from Edgar Ray Killen that this was an organization of action. This was no Boy Scout group, it was here to do business. ... Dennis, who had left the Klan, was asked to re-enter and to penetrate the heart of the secret organization, and that he did. Members of the Jury, the payment for information that these informers received for the risk they took, for the time they consumed, for the expenses they incurred for the inevitable isolation when their role came out is pretty meager. Their payment was made for value received. These men are not criminals, they played no part in this or any other conspiracy, and for the FBI there was no other way to proceed. So, I come here now to ask only that you do justice. ... This was a small, secret militant group, masterminded by a fanatic, who had singled out Schwerner as a man who had to be eliminated—not to preserve or protect Mississippi, but rather to satisfy his own consuming hate."

Of all those who testified that day, the most powerful witness was James Jordan, who testified at length about the case. When asked about being contacted by Killen, he told the jurors, "Well, he went in and talked to Frank Herndon first then he came back out and said he had a job he needed some help on over in Neshoba County and he needed some men to go with him. He said that two or three of those civil rights workers were locked up and they needed their rear ends tore up. ... Well several more calls were made and at that time they said they had two or three men on the way, and asked me if I knew a couple that we might get, that we needed about six or seven men. ...we needed some gloves and I asked to stop by and see if I could find any gloves, any rubber gloves, which I couldn't at the time. We stopped at Warren's Grocery Store on the way to Wayne's house. ... I asked [Wayne] if he could go, that they needed some help on a case in Neshoba County, and that Reverend Killen was down and could he get away to go? ... Mr. Akins was there, Pete Harris was, myself, Wayne at that time, then he said there were some more boys on their way which they arrived in just a few minutes. ... Well at that time Reverend Killen said they had three of the Civil Rights Workers locked up and we had to hurry and get there and we were to pick them up and tear their butts up. He said that a Highway Patrol car would stop them on the outskirts of town. ... He said he would go ahead as he had to get on back there as fast as he could and make the arrangements, there were several cars were coming in and these guys couldn't be held much longer."

Later in his testimony, Jordan described the police's involvement in the crimes: "We left and drove our highway 19 back toward Meridian. At that time there was a red car ahead of us and that's what we did, a red Chevrolet. There was some more men in it. We came back out to the outskirts of Philadelphia. The red car pulled over beside a Highway Patrol car and we pulled up behind it. The man driving the red car got out and said something to the Patrol car and he walked back to our car and said, 'never mind, they will stopped by the Deputy Sheriff, these men are not going to stop them.' ... About that time the Deputy's car came by, said something to the man in the red car, and the Deputy's car, and we took off to follow them. ... Well, we were following the red car as we were told to do, we got on down the highways a good ways, the car broke down. Evidently it broke down, it stopped beside the road. We stopped behind it. Posey told us to come on and go ahead that it would be stopped anyway by the Sheriff, the Deputy Sheriff, and we were to follow them. He got in the car with us and left this young man there to try and fix his car. We went on back toward Meridian from Philadelphia to a cut-off highway, I don't know which number it is, toward Union, and we were traveling at a pretty high rate of speed and about that time we caught the tail end of the Deputy's car ahead of us. We saw a little wagon in front of him which he had pulled over to the side of the road."

This, of course, was the CORE station wagon.

Jordan continued with testimony about the grim details of the trio's final minutes: "We pulled up behind him, he got out and went up and told the three men that were in the car to get out. ... They got in the back of his car and Posey told Arledge to get in their car and follow them and we turned and went back. ...I heard a thump like the Deputy was rushing them up to get in there or where he hit one of them or the car or what, but I did hear a thump. ... [Leaving, we] Turned left on highway 19 all the way to, oh about 34 miles to this other cut-off road which wasn't a paved highway and then they said somebody had better stay here and watch in case anything happens, 'til the other car comes. ... We turned left off the highway [on to] a graded clay road. I got out of the car to watch and see if anything was happening, and the other cars proceeded on up the road. Well, I hear a car door slamming, and some loud talking, I couldn't understand or distinguish anybody's voice or anything, and then I heard several shots. Walked up the road toward where the noise came from. Just a bunch of men milling and standing around that had been in the two cars ahead of us and someone said, 'better pick up these shells.' I hollered, 'what do you want me to do?' ... We put [the bodies] through the back window of the truck lid of their wagon. ... At that time the Highway Deputy, or the Deputy Sheriff's car turned around and went back toward Highway 19, Posey said, 'just follow me, I know where we're going.'"

Finally, Jordan gave his version of the burial of the bodies: "We went through a barbwire fence and was there. [I] opened the back of the station wagon, took the boys out and took them down in this hollow. ... Posey told us to go back up the road and listen out that the operator was not there yet so Jim Snowden and I walked back up the road to wait. Then at that time we thought we heard something coming through the woods but it was nothing but a cow and about that time he said Doyle and Raymond Sharpe were going to find the bulldozer operator because he wasn't there when we got there so they left to go and get him. Well they came back in a different way they did not come back in by us at that time and we heard someone whistle across the way and Snowden said, 'I'll go see who it is' and he walked down the road just a little ways, came back and said it must be the operator and about that time we heard the bulldozer crank up. [After they were buried] We got back in the car and then we were going to put the license plate back on it which had been taken off of Doyle Barnett's car. Posey told us we could go back to this place and put the license plate back on the car and Sharpe knew the was to come round the road and that he would wait there and take the operator back. He said the station wagon, don't worry about it it would be taken to Alabama and be burned. ... He said, 'Herman will take it to Alabama' is all I know."

Doar also read the jury Barnette's recanted confession, and the stories those two men told were so similar in their details that it seemed impossible they could be lying. Though the defense would put up a few specious arguments, based primarily on character witnesses and questionable alibis, Doar knew that the testimony was on his side. The only question was whether the jury would actually convict their own of killing three despised outsiders. In his final summation, he reminded them, "Members of the Jury, this is an important case. It is important to the government. It's important to the defendants, but most important, it's important to the State of

Mississippi. What I say, what the other lawyers say here today, what the Court says about the law will soon be forgotten, but what you twelve people do here today will long be remembered. These defendants will stand before you on the record in this case and they will beg of you for indulgence. In effect they will say as Gloucester said as he stood over the body of his slain king, 'Say I slew him not.' The queen replied, 'Then say they were not slain.' But they are dead. If you find that these men are not guilty of this conspiracy it would be as true to say that there was no nighttime release from jail by Cecil Price, there were no White Knights, there are no young men dead, there was no murder. If you find that these men are not guilty, you will declare the law of Neshoba County to be the law of the State of Mississippi."

The jury received the case at 4:24 p.m. on October 18, and they deliberated for three hours before retiring for the night. The next day, they returned to the courtroom and informed the judge that they were deadlocked. Cox sent them back to the jury room with a stern reminder that trials were expensive and that they had a responsibility to make a decision.

The jury obeyed him and returned the next morning to announce their decision. They found the following men guilty: Cecil Ray Price, Jimmy Arledge, Sam Bowers, Wayne Roberts, Jimmy Snowden, Billy Wayne Posey and Horace Doyle Barnette. They remained deadlocked about Killen, Sharpe and Ethel Glen Barnett. They acquitted everyone else, including Rainey, Burrage and Akin.

With that, Cox sentenced Roberts and Bowers to 10 years each and the others involved to shorter sentences of either five or three years. He later said, "They killed one n*****, one Jew, and a white man. I gave them all what I thought they deserved." Though these were hardly just sentences in a "hang'em high" state like Mississippi, Doar was still pleased with the results: "To have that jury return that verdict was a great thing. The jury paid attention; they were serious people. …they were applying the beyond-a-reasonable-doubt standard very strictly. …the trial helped Mississippi get beyond the caste system. Up to that time, no white person in the state had ever been convicted for violence against a black. After the trial, the good people of Mississippi became more confident that they could move away from their past."

The government decided not to retry Killen, Sharpe, and Barnett, as it was thought that the convictions were the best that could be gotten in Mississippi at the time. As a result, Killen, arguably the man most responsible for the deaths, remained free for the next 45 years.

As the case was ongoing, *The Saturday Evening Post* captured the essence of what brought about the crimes in the first place: "Deep angers and frustrations now motivate the Klansman. He is rebelling against his own ignorance, ignorance that restricts him to the hard and poorly paid jobs that are becoming scarcer every day. He is angered by the knowledge that the world is passing him by, that he is sinking lower and lower in the social order. The Negro is his scapegoat, for he knows that so long as the Negro can be kept 'in his place,' there will be somebody on the social and economic scale who is lower than be. In the Klavern in his robes, repeating the ancient ritual, he finds the status that is denied him on the outside."

Fortunately, those kinds of attitudes changed over the ensuing decades, and after years of calls for the reopening of the Mississippi Burning Case and retrying Killen, the 80 year old segregationist was arrested in 2004 on three counts of murder. In 2005, Edgar Ray Killen was convicted of three counts of manslaughter and sentenced to 60 years in prison. He is still serving his sentence at the Mississippi State Penitentiary in Parchman.

Online Resources

Other titles about the Civil Rights Movement by Charles River Editors

Other titles about 20th century history by Charles River Editors

Other titles about the murders on Amazon

Bibliography

Mississippi Burning, by Joel Norst. New American Library, 1988.

The "Mississippi Burning" Civil Rights Murder Conspiracy Trial: A Headline Court Case, by Harvey Fireside. Enslow Publishers, 2002.

The Mississippi Burning Trial: A Primary Source Account, by Bill Scheppler. The Rosen Publishing Group, 2003.

Three Lives for Mississippi, by William Bradford Huie. University Press of Mississippi, 1965.

We Are Not Afraid, by Seth Cagin and Philip Dray. Bantam Books, 1988.

Witness in Philadelphia, by Florence Mars. Louisiana State University Press, 1977.

Made in United States
North Haven, CT
27 May 2024

52893520R00026